# GREEN PATROL

**Leader:** Martha Singh (supported by Olive Summer)

**Age:** 13

**Status:** Billionaire

**Company name:** HALO

## GREEN PATROL MEMBERS

AYAN

MAX

SILVA

SHAN

**HALO's objective:** To carry on the work that Martha's missing mum and dad started – to save wildlife and to save the planet.

**Enemy target:** TITAN (HALO's enemy). TITAN is a big company that puts wildlife and the environment at risk. It makes money from environmental crime.

Is TITAN behind Martha's missing mum and dad …?

**Next task:** Code name: **Alps**

# Chapter 1

*Hong Kong, China ...*

Shan saw the first crate emerge. It was marked with a sticker that said **TITAN: TAKE CARE!** It was loaded on to a huge cargo plane. The plane would leave soon, for France. Three more crates followed. Each crate held an endangered snow leopard.

HALO

# GREEN PATROL

## ALPS

Written by Bali Rai
Illustrated by Margherita Ende

RISING STARS

Hachette UK's policy is to use papers that are natural, renewable and recyclable products and made from wood grown in well-managed forests and other controlled sources. The logging and manufacturing processes are expected to conform to the environmental regulations of the country of origin.

**ISBN: 9781398324282**


First published in 2021 by Hodder & Stoughton Limited (for its Rising Stars imprint, part of the Hodder Education Group),
An Hachette UK Company
Carmelite House, 50 Victoria Embankment, London EC4Y 0DZ
www.risingstars-uk.com

Impression number 10 9 8 7 6 5 4 3 2 1
Year 2025 2024 2023 2022 2021

Author: Bali Rai
Series Editor: Tony Bradman
Commissioning Editor: Hamish Baxter
Illustrator: Margherita Ende/Astound US
Educational Reviewer: Helen Marron
Design concept: Julie Joubinaux
Page layout: Rocket Design (East Anglia) Ltd
Editor: Amy Tyrer

With thanks to the schools that took part in the development of *Reading Planet* KS2, including: Ancaster CE Primary School, Ancaster; Downsway Primary School, Reading; Ferry Lane Primary School, London; Foxborough Primary School, Slough; Griffin Park Primary School, Blackburn; St Barnabas CE First & Middle School, Pershore; Tranmoor Primary School, Doncaster; and Wilton CE Primary School, Wilton.



A catalogue record for this title is available from the British Library.

Printed in the United Kingdom.

Orders: Please contact Hachette UK Distribution, Hely Hutchinson Centre, Milton Road, Didcot, Oxfordshire, OX11 7HH.

Telephone: (44) 01235 400555. Email: primary@hachette.co.uk.

FSC www.fsc.org MIX Paper from responsible sources FSC™ C104740

The private airport was quiet. Shan and Olive watched from a warehouse. They had to stay hidden.

"What shall we do?" Shan asked Olive.

"We wait," said Olive.

Shan felt helpless. "Can't we just stop them?" she asked.

"No," Olive replied. "We need to stop the person behind this or they will just try again."

"So, we follow their plane?" asked Shan.

"Not follow," Olive replied. "That would give the game away. We'll track them."

Shan nodded. "Cool," she replied.

"Besides, we are Green Patrol," said Olive. "We *like* a challenge!"

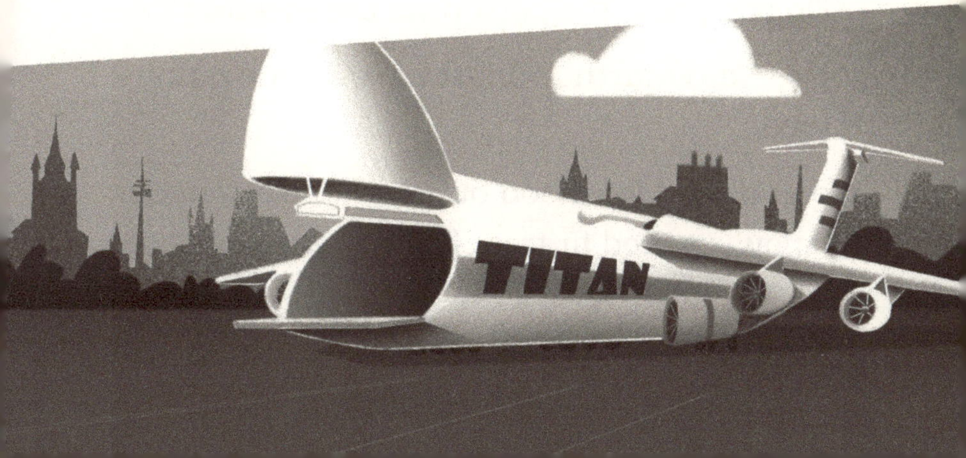

# Chapter 2

*One day later ... a city near the Alps, France ...*

Green Patrol had split into pairs. Martha and Max were waiting to meet a contact. Ayan was with Silva, keeping watch on a suspect. Olive and Shan were travelling to the Alps from Hong Kong.

Olive contacted Martha on her HALO phone. "Are we all in place?" she asked.

"All in place," Martha replied. "Keep in contact."

Max looked at his HALO phone.

"Do you know the person we are meeting?"

"No," said Martha. "I just have a code name – Lynx ..."

Soon after, Max stood out on the street, under a snow-covered fir tree. The city was divided by a massive river. He wore ear buds, which allowed him to hear and speak to Martha. She was across the river.

"Has Lynx made contact yet?" asked Martha.

It was getting dark and cold. Max shivered. Snow had begun to fall. "Nothing yet," he told Martha. "How much longer?"

Martha was cold, too. She stood beside a bridge that crossed the river. "Hang on," she told Max. "Let me track Lynx on my HALO phone ..."

"... Lynx should be near!" she told Max.

# Chapter 3

*St Leon, the Alps, France ...*

Ayan's cheeks and nose were bright red from the cold. The landscape was stunning – the lake, the little town of St Leon, and the mountain. Their boat sat in the middle of the lake.

"It's so pretty in the snow," said Ayan as the sun went down.

"Too cold," Silva replied through chattering teeth.

Deep in the shadow of the mountain was a house. Not any old house. It was like a palace made of glass and metal. "Wow," gasped Ayan. "What a place to live!"

Silva showed her his HALO phone. “Lady Varon lives there,” he said. “She’s our target!”

“I’ve seen the file,” said Ayan. “She is a powerful member of TITAN.”

Green Patrol were getting used to facing danger. Lady Varon would be their most difficult test yet.

“So, do we sit, watch and follow?” Silva asked.

“Yes,” Ayan replied. “You really should have worn another jacket.”

Silva scowled.

“Hang on!” Ayan cried. “Target in sight.”

Silva used his HALO phone to zoom in ...

On the shore, they saw two big men, dressed in black. With them was a woman, dressed all in white. “That’s Lady Varon,” said Silva. “She’s on the move!”

# Chapter 4

*HALO's jet, somewhere over the Alps ...*

Shan loved the HALO jet plane. It was packed with gadgets – computers and scanners and all sorts. It had a shower, a film room and even a games console. Shan loved to play games!

Shan pointed at a screen. "What's this for?" she asked Olive.

"Leave it alone, dear," said Olive. "You might damage something."

Shan grinned and swiped the screen.

The screen woke up to show three live camera feeds. "What are we looking at?" Shan asked.

Olive tapped the screen three times. "Martha and Max are there," she said. "Ayan and Silva are over there. And the plane we're tracking is here."

"Cool!" said Shan.

Suddenly, a high-pitched alarm went off. There was a very loud bang. The plane began to shake and shudder.

Olive ran to a locker. She took out two backpacks. "STRAP IN!" she shouted.

Shan flung on the backpack and Olive grabbed a cord at the side of her own pack.

"WATCH ME!" she shouted. "DO EXACTLY WHAT I DO!"

"WHY?" yelled Shan.

"BECAUSE WE HAVE TO JUMP OUT!" Olive screamed. "THE PLANE IS GOING DOWN ..."

# Chapter 5

*A city near the Alps, France ...*

Max saw Lynx. She was tall, probably in her 30s and wore a long, black coat.

"You are just a child!" she glared at Max. "What is HALO doing? TITAN isn't scared of children!"

Max smiled. "They should be," he told her.

"Make the swap," she said. "I don't wish to get found out."

Max handed a package to Lynx, just as he had been told to.

"And here is your key," said Lynx. "This will help you to hack TITAN's computers."

She gave Max a USB stick. Then she left without another word.

“Bye!” said Max.

He waited a moment before contacting Martha again. “The swap is complete,” he told her. “Can we get out of the cold now?”

“No,” said Martha. “Now, we join Ayan and Silva.”

“But …?” said Max.

“We rest when the job is finished,” Martha told him.

“Oh, brilliant!” Max replied. “I’ll just freeze then …”

# Chapter 6

*St Leon, the Alps ...*

Lady Varon was on the move. Her boat was fast, but so was the HALO boat. Ayan and Silva had been trained to drive it and were experts in high-speed chases. Green Patrol were kids with skills!

"I wonder where she's going?" said Ayan.

"Maybe the snow leopards are here?" replied Silva.

They kept behind Lady Varon until her boat reached the town of St Leon.

At the dock, Lady Varon jumped out. A car was waiting. She got in and drove away at speed.

Silva tried to call Olive, but there was no reply. "That's odd," he said.

He tried Martha.

"We've lost Lady Varon," said Silva. "And it's getting dark."

"Olive should be able to track her," Martha replied.

"She's not replying," said Silva.

"Hmm, strange ..." said Martha.

Ayan steered the boat into the dock at St Leon. "There's only one road out of town," Silva told Martha. "So we know which way Lady Varon is going."

"Yes," said Martha. "But *where* is she going?"

"And *why?*" asked Ayan.

# Chapter 7

*Somewhere in the mountains ...*

Shan slowly stood up. Her legs were wobbly. She had seen Olive and the pilot parachute away from the plane, but the HALO jet had been destroyed.

It was cold and dark. The ground was covered in fresh snow. Shan's face, hands and feet had lost all feeling. "Olive!" she shouted.

She searched for her HALO phone, but it was gone. "OLIVE!!!!!"

Shan began to trudge down the mountain. Suddenly, she saw two lights coming towards her. A car.

...

Olive had jumped from the plane with Shan, but had lost sight of her in the fall.

The pilot was missing, too. All three of them had escaped, but now they were still in danger. It was dark and the snow was thick. Unless they found shelter, they were going to struggle.

If only she could speak to Martha.

Olive tried to work out what had happened. The HALO plane should not have crashed. It was odd. There had to be a reason.

"TITAN!" Olive exclaimed. "They must be behind this!"

In the distance, Olive saw two lights moving towards her. A car ...

# Chapter 8

*St Leon, the Alps ...*

Martha and Max arrived in St Leon by HALO helicopter. Every building was covered in snow. On a normal night, it would have felt very pretty. But this was not a normal night.

"We're here!" said Martha, speaking through her HALO phone. "Are you still at the dock?"

"Yes," Ayan replied.

"Have you heard from Olive and Shan?" asked Max.

"No," Silva told him. "No word at all."

"Olive would never stay silent," Martha told Max. "They are in trouble."

"Yes," Max replied. "But what trouble?"

"It must be TITAN," Martha said.

A short while later, Martha and Max met up with Ayan and Silva.

"Can we still track the snow leopards?" asked Ayan.

"But we can't just forget Olive and Shan," protested Silva.

"We have no choice," said Max. "Olive will find a way ..."

"Perhaps I can be of help?" said a voice from the darkness.

Green Patrol turned to find a woman behind them.

"Hello," she said. "I'm Agent Sharp."

The four children looked around nervously.

"Don't worry, I'm here to help you," Agent Sharp smiled. "I've been watching you since your last job in Brazil ..."

# Chapter 9

*Somewhere in the mountains ...*

Back on the mountain, Shan watched the car come slowly closer. It was big and shiny with huge wheels. It had begun to snow again. She had no coat and no phone. She couldn't stay outside.

As the car stopped, Shan began to feel better. She was lucky. A door opened and a woman stepped out. She wore a white fur coat and

white snow boots. Her face was hidden by a thick, white scarf. Shan could only see her eyes.

"You had better get in."

Shan did as she was told. The car was warm and cosy. The woman poured Shan a steaming cup of hot chocolate from a steel flask.

"Who are you?" Shan asked again.

The woman removed her scarf. Shan gasped.

...

When the shiny white car pulled up and the woman in the white coat got out, Olive also felt that she had no choice.

She got in and came face to face with a surprised-looking Shan.

"Olive!" she shouted, hugging her.

The woman closed the door and poured some more hot chocolate from her flask.

"How did you find us ... *Lady Varon*?" Olive asked her.

"That was easy," said Lady Varon. "Your parachutes were bugged, so I could tell where you would land."

Shan scowled.

Olive just smiled. "But how did you bring the plane down?"

A black screen divided the driver from the rest of the passengers. Lady Varon pushed a button. The screen came down and they saw the HALO pilot sitting in the front. Shan and Olive gasped in shock. The HALO pilot worked for TITAN ...

# Chapter 10

*St Leon, the Alps ...*

Agent Sharp explained that she was part of a secret group. Like HALO, they had been watching TITAN for a very long time.

"We know about Green Patrol. We like what you do."

"So, why all the secrets?" asked Max.

"Secrets are our thing," Agent Sharp replied. She grinned, and Martha did, too.

"So, you want to help us?" said Ayan.

"Yes," said Agent Sharp.

"Do you know where Olive and Shan are?" asked Silva.

"Yes," she told him.

"Where?" asked Martha eagerly.

When Agent Sharp told them, Ayan and Silva were shocked.

"You let TITAN take our friends?" Max shouted.

"We could not stop them," Agent Sharp told him. "We must catch Lady Varon. She has important knowledge that we need."

Agent Sharp called for a car. "Lady Varon has a secret base," she said. "Up in the mountains."

Martha nodded and showed Agent Sharp the USB stick from Lynx. "This has the code to Lady Varon's secret base."

"Perfect!" said Agent Sharp. "We are going to rescue your friends and catch Lady Varon!"

*"Then,"* she said, "I have a job for Green Patrol. A *big* job."

# Chapter 11

*Lady Varon's mountain base ...*

Lady Varon pointed at the mountain ahead. All Shan could see was a huge lump of rock with ice and snow all over it.

"That is my base," she said. "You would never have found it!"

Lady Varon took out a phone and tapped the screen a few times. A moment later, the side of the mountain opened to show a tunnel ...

"Wow!" said Shan. "That is kind of cool."

"TITAN is *very* cool," Lady Varon replied. "You should have chosen to be on our side."

"It's okay," said Shan. "I'm happy with HALO, thanks."

Lady Varon took Olive and Shan to a lift and up to Level 3.

They passed by an enormous swimming pool. Down a corridor, they saw many rooms on both sides.

Lady Varon looked into a scanner by a door. The door slid open. The room was huge, with two white sofas, a glass table and a giant widescreen TV.

"Get used to the place. You will be here for a long time ..." she said, nodding to the large, angry-looking man guarding the door.

# Chapter 12

*In the mountains near Lady Varon's base ...*

The sun was starting to rise as Agent Sharp stopped the car close to Lady Varon's mountain base.

Agent Sharp turned to Green Patrol. "Who is the best hacker?" she asked.

"Ayan," they all replied.

Martha handed the USB stick to Ayan. Agent Sharp gave her a laptop. Ayan connected the USB stick and began to tap the keyboard.

"How long will it take?" asked Agent Sharp.

"Not long at all," said Ayan.

Agent Sharp turned to Martha. "Is your team ready?"

"Green Patrol is ready," Martha replied.

"Marvellous," said Agent Sharp.

She gave phones to Max, Silva and Martha. A few moments later, Ayan cleared her throat.

"I am in," she told them all.

Agent Sharp checked the laptop. "Wow," she said to Ayan. "You *are* good!"

"The best!" Ayan replied, grinning.

"Lady Varon has sensors and cameras to protect the base," said Agent Sharp. "Can you turn them off?"

Ayan tapped the keyboard again. "Okay. All off now." she said.

"Time to move, then," said Martha.

# Chapter 13

*Lady Varon's mountain base ...*

Inside the base, the team split up. Martha and Silva's job was to stop Lady Varon. Max was to find and rescue Shan and Olive. Agent Sharp and Ayan would stay outside and tell them where to go through their ear buds.

"Go to the lift," Ayan said to Max. "I'll open it for you."

Max sprinted to the lift. Once inside, he waited.

"Level 3," Ayan told him. "Turn left and follow the corridor."

The lift began to move. At Level 3, the doors slid open. Max was shocked by what he found ...

“Wow!” he said. “This place is *so* cool. There’s even a swimming pool!”

“Stick to the job,” said Agent Sharp.

Max followed the corridor, as asked. He moved quickly and quietly. Soon, Ayan told him to stop.

“I can see two doors,” said Max.

“Hang on,” said Ayan.

Max stood, silently waiting ... suddenly a hand grabbed him from behind! He yelled out in surprise.

“Max?” said Ayan.

Max did not reply.

...

Martha and Silva found Lady Varon on the first floor. She was sitting in a control room, talking to a man on the screen. A sad snow leopard appeared on the screen.

"The customers are ready," said the man's voice.

Martha whispered into her phone. "What do we do?" she asked.

"Let her begin her sale," Agent Sharp replied.

"But we came to save the leopards," said Silva.

"I promise they will be saved, but for now, we need Lady Varon ..."

"NO!" yelled Silva.

Lady Varon turned in shock. "You meddling brats!" she cried. She hit a button on the desk, and the room suddenly went dark.

Lady Varon jumped up and ran.

# Chapter 14

Max spun around to see Shan standing in the corridor of Level 3.

"Shan!" Max gasped. "You scared me! How did you get away?"

Shan shrugged. "Easy. Lady Varon's guard was working undercover for HALO. He let us out."

Suddenly, the base went dark. Doors began to slam shut and Olive came running down the corridor. "GET OUT!" she yelled. "NOW!"

They all sprinted for the lift. But they were too late, it had been shut down.

*"AYAN!"* Max shouted into his HALO phone. "What's happening? I've got Shan and Olive here," he said.

"She's locking the base down," Ayan said.

"You need to get out or you will be sealed inside the mountain!"

Lady Varon took the stairs. She was heading for the exit on the ground floor. All across the base, every door was being locked down. Soon, there would be no escape.

"STOP HER!" yelled Agent Sharp.

Silva and Martha burst on to the stairs and jumped down them.

They saw Lady Varon leap on to a scooter. She zoomed off towards the exit. More scooters were parked outside. Silva and Martha each took one and set off after Lady Varon ...

# Chapter 15

Back on Level 3, Max, Shan and Olive were trapped.

"Ayan!" shouted Max through his HALO phone. "Help us!"

"Stay cool," said Ayan. "I have another idea. Go to the swimming pool."

Green Patrol sprinted past the pool, and then they saw it – a gap in the wall – a hole in the side of the mountain. Through two large open doors was a ledge with something on it ...

"No way!" said Max.

"Hang-gliders," Shan replied. "This is going to be *so* cool!"

Olive strapped Shan and Max into their gliders. Then she picked one for herself.

"GO!" she yelled.

They took a few steps and jumped off the ledge into the snowy morning haze ...

Meanwhile, Lady Varon sped through the tunnel exit, just as it began to close. Martha and Silva were close behind.

"We're not going to make it!" Martha screamed.

Just before the door slammed shut, they slid out into the snowstorm. The scooters were useless in the snow. As Martha and Silva slid across towards her, Lady Varon tried to go faster. BIG mistake! Her scooter flipped, throwing her up into the air and then down into the snow.

Martha and Silva got to Lady Varon just as Agent Sharp's car arrived.

Lady Varon lay splayed out in the snow. "You horrible, meddling kids!" she yelled at them. "How dare you do this to me!"

Swooping down on the hang-gliders, Olive, Max and Shan landed close by. Martha grinned.

Lady Varon seemed confused. "Do you know who I am?" she said.

"Yes," said Martha.

"Then you know I can't be stopped," said Lady Varon. "TITAN can't be stopped. You're just a bunch of kids!"

"We're not just kids," Martha replied. "We're Green Patrol!"

# Chapter 16

*Wiston Hall, England …*

As Green Patrol ate pizza, Agent Sharp appeared on the large screen in Martha's kitchen.

"Hey, kids," she said. "Brilliant work, catching Lady Varon. She's been locked up."

"What about the snow leopards?" asked Silva.

"We rescued them," Agent Sharp replied. "They are all safe."

"You got back into the mountain base?" asked Shan.

"With Lady Varon's help," said Agent Sharp. "She's proved to be *very useful.*" Agent Sharp hesitated. "We discovered something else on the USB stick, too …" she said.

"What was that?" asked Ayan.

"I'll leave that to Martha to explain," said Agent Sharp. "I've sent her a message. See you soon, kids."

Martha checked her HALO phone.

"So?" Ayan said. "Can we rest now?"

"Not yet," replied Martha. "Agent Sharp has a big problem. She needs our help."

"It never ends, but we'll be ready," said Max.

Martha smiled. "The USB stick had a folder about my parents," she announced. "They might be alive ..."

"What?!" Shan yelled, jumping up. "That's amazing news!"

"Yeah," said Martha. "I really hope so. Maybe we can find them ..."

"We will!" said Ayan. "We are Green Patrol. We never stop. And we *never give up!*"

## Chat about the book

1 Where is the setting for the part of the story in Chapter 2?

2 Read page 26. What did Lady Varon mean when she said, "Get used to the place. You will be here for a long time ..."?

3 Read Chapter 9. How was Shan feeling at different points in this chapter?

4 The author does not want us to like Lady Varon. How does the author do this?

5 Go to page 33 and 34. Why did the author use 'burst', 'leap' and 'zoomed' in this part of the story?

6 The members of Green Patrol were sometimes in danger. Do you like books like this?